EXPLORING QUANTITY FOOD PRODUCTION AND SERVICE THROUGH PROBLEMS

Second Edition

Elizabeth McKinney Lieux
Patricia Kelly Luoto

Prentice Hall
Upper Saddle River, New Jersey 07458

Acquisitions Editor: *Neil Marquardt*
Director of Manufacturing and Production: *Bruce Johnson*
Managing Editor: *Mary Carnis*
Manufacturing Buyer: *Ed O'Dougherty*
Production Editor: *Denise Brown*
Printer/Binder: *Banta Harrisonburg*
Creative Director: *Marianne Frasco*
Senior Design Coordinator: *Miguel Ortiz*
Marketing Manager: *Shannon Simonsen*

Printed in the United States of America

10 9 8 7 6 5 4 3 2

ISBN 0-13-083534-X

Prentice-Hall International (UK) Limited, *London*
Prentice-Hall of Australia Pty. Limited, *Sydney*
Prentice-Hall Canada Inc., *Toronto*
Prentice-Hall Hispanoamericana, S.A., *Mexico*
Prentice-Hall of India Private Limited, *New Delhi*
Prentice-Hall of Japan, Inc., *Tokyo*
Prentice-Hall Pte. Ltd., *Singapore*
Editora Prentice-Hall do Brasil, Ltda., *Rio de Janeiro*

CONTENTS

ACKNOWLEDGMENTS

The authors wish to thank Kim Doherty, MA, RD, Child Nutrition Supervisor, Brandywine School, Wilmington DE, for her help in creating the problems related to school breakfast and lunch programs. Barbara Duch, MA, of the University of Delaware helped refine the problems and contributed mightily to our understanding of Problem-based Learning.

We have asked the advice of many colleagues who have graciously provided us with wonderful assistance. We also thank the hundreds of our students who have explored Quantity Food Production and Service with us utilizing these problems. They gave the benefit of the doubt in this new way to learn and demonstrated to us that active learning in teams is not only possible but beneficial to acquisition, application and retention of knowledge.

Course Description

This course was designed to allow students the opportunity to learn Quantity Food Production and Service by confronting problem narratives. Students search fo underlying principles and concepts as they research each problem. Through completing worksheets, consulting reference materials, and group discussions students learn the important foodservice principles which guide dietitian's and foodservice manager's practice.

Companion Textbook

Payne-Palacio J., Theis M: *West and Wood's: Introduction to Foodservice*, 8th edition, New York: Merrill, Prentice Hall Company, 1997.
OR
Spears M: *Foodservice Organizations*, 4th edition, Englewood Cliffs, NJ, Merrill, Prentice Hall Company, 1999.

Course Expectations and Student Responsibilities in a Problem-Based Learning (PBL) Course

The underlying belief of PBL is that learning is more meaningful and enjoyable when it occurs in small groups which are self-directed. Research has shown that material learned when the learner is actively involved is retained much longer. Additionally, when learning is in context rather than as a series of isolated facts and theories, the concepts are retained better. A framework of expectations will be provided, but within that framework students assume responsibility for their own learning and that of their learning group.

Students work in small groups on problems assigned by the instructor. It is expected that students will work together on the problems to identify what they already know and then identify the **learning issues** which need to be explored to understand the problem. A list of learning issues will be generated and prioritized for each problem. At the end of each class session the group will decide how best to acquire the information needed to understand the problem. The group will assign learning issues to members of the group. Each member of the group will locate at least one useful and pertinent reference to share with the group for each problem. At the next class meeting the students will report **orally** their research results and all will discuss the information gathered. When the group and the instructor are satisfied that the objectives for the problem have been achieved, another problem is taken for study. In some instances more than one member of the group may work on the same learning issues. At other times each member will investigate different issues. Members of the group will identify which resources were consulted so these may be documented in the problem write-up.

In this course a minimum of **nine hours** per week in outside preparation time is needed. In most cases it is not necessary to hold group meetings outside of class. Outside preparation is for the purpose of individual research on the assigned learning issues and individual responsibility for worksheets or problem write-ups.

Course Objectives

There are two kinds of objectives in a PBL course: **Process objectives** (HOW to learn) and **Content objectives** (WHAT to learn).

Process objectives: Given a problem in foodservice systems management, the student will:
- generate learning issues
- organize relevant issues into learning tasks
- research appropriate information from a variety of sources. (The textbook is the principle resource. Other appropriate sources include: journals, periodicals, books, credible resource persons, the Internet, data bases.)
- critically analyze the information obtained
- synthesize the information into a coherent framework
- share the information obtained
- apply research findings to solution of problems
- facilitate learning of the others in the group

Content objectives: Students will utilize foodservice management theory and resources to discover principles about the production and service of food in large organizations. This investigation will include the scope of the foodservice industry, food safety, menu planning, purchasing and inventory control, controlling production, delivery and service systems, and the financial impact of management decisions.

Class Policies in a PBL Class

Attendance at each class session is **mandatory** since the group learning requires each member to be present. However, if absence is necessary the student is responsible for contacting each group member in advance. All research materials should be provided for each group member before the class and the absent member will be available either by way of e-mail or telephone to respond to questions. It is also necessary to communicate after the class to find out assignments for the next session.

Group Work and Class Organization

The class will be divided into groups. Assignment to the groups is made by the instructor. Groups are **permanent** for the entire semester as would be found in the working world. It is essential for everyone in the group to contribute to the group effort. In order to ensure everyone's participation, roles will be assigned which will rotate with each problem.

The description of responsibility for possible roles follows:
- **Discussion leader:** Reads the problem out loud. Responsible for moving the group forward in accomplishing the assignment. Keeps discussion on track. Assures that all members of the group contribute to the discussion. Aids the group in summarizing conclusions.
- **Scribe:** Responsible for recording data and notes on discussions. Records initial problem solving strategies. Develops list of resources used. Keeps notes on the

discussion and on the assignment of tasks and learning issues.

- **Reporter**: Uses information developed by scribe to create write-up of problem. May provide oral reports to entire class.
- **Accuracy coach**: Responsible for checking text and notes for accuracy of discussions during problem solving sessions. Responsible for questioning all group members on their understanding of concepts.
- **Skeptic**: Responsible for functioning as "Devil's Advocate." Should suggest alternate solutions and sometimes introduce controversial elements into the discussion.

Group Rules: Each group will develop its own ground rules for behavior. Group rules are to be written and provided to each group member and the instructor. Rules may be modified as necessary with group consensus. The following rules are suggested:

- Attendance is mandatory. If a member is absent it hinders group learning.
- Come to class prepared. It is each member's responsibility to be ready to contribute to the group effort. Each is responsible for locating at least one appropriate reference for each problem.
- Fulfill the role responsibility. The discussion leader keeps the group working on the problem. The accuracy coach brings the text and notes, etc.
- Members of the group should show respect for the contributions and opinions of the other group members. Although disagreements and differences of opinion are expected and welcome, members should treat other group members respectfully. No disrespectful comments are allowed.
- Other rules which the group believes are appropriate and necessary for good group functioning.

The group should decide in advance the **consequences** of not adhering to each of the ground rules. Peer evaluations may be used to censure members who do not follow the agreed upon rules. Suspension or expulsion from the group are possible consequences of repeated violations of the group rules.

Evaluation and Feedback

Upon completion of each problem group members will provide informal feedback on the performance of all members that week. This feedback should focus on what each member did to help the learning process and what each member could do differently to help the group. Statements should be made constructively and positively. For example: Poor feedback = "You are too bossy." Good feedback = "I like to help make decisions about the direction we are going." Poor feedback = "Don't just copy pages of material for each person." Good feedback = "I learn more when you explain what you read instead of giving us the copies to read ourselves."

Two times during the semester a formal written evaluation of the members of the group will be completed. These evaluations will be part of each individual's grade. Evaluation forms to be used may be found on beginning on Page 129 and should be consulted weekly as a guide for the informal feedback. In addition, at the end of the course the instructor will be completing an evaluation of each individual using similar criteria. The instructor will provide a summary of peer comments and a grade for the student evaluations.

Suggestions

Research has shown that students who study in groups learn better and perform better than students who work on their own. Problem-based Learning and reliance on a team of learners may be a new experience to some group members. Success will be assured if each group member completes the assigned research carefully and completely and shares what was learned with the group.

Course Components

A number of activities are planned. A worksheet has been developed for each problem which focuses specifically on content central to the problem under study. Worksheets are to be completed individually prior to tackling the problem to provide background knowledge for the PBL process.

There will be a new problem to address each week. Learning in each will be assessed through quizzes and write-ups. The instructor will provide a wrap-up of each problem to summarize major concepts. There may be whole class discussion or oral reports. Ultimately each member of the group is responsible for understanding the material from each assigned chapter in the textbook.

Resources to be Used

The most frequently used resource is one of the two companion textbooks. Both provide valuable information for the worksheets and the problems. Additional resources in the form of articles and books will be made available for each problem by the instructor. The Web page of one of the authors provides many useful resources which are appropriate for each problem. http://copland.udel.edu/~lieux/companion/companion.htm Students may also consult recognized authorities in appropriate disciplines who can offer valuable perspectives.

Problem Write-ups

All problem write-ups will be word processed or typed. Write-ups should include all relevant information to demonstrate a comprehensive understanding of the learning issues while demonstrating brevity and an economy of effort. The write-ups should not exceed four typed pages. Include a Problem Write-Up Evaluation Form (pg. 121) with each write-up. Only the evaluation form will be returned.

The following information will be provided:
- List of learning issues identified.

- Discussion of each learning issue identifying what the group has learned. References should be utilized and incorporated into the discussion.
- Conclusion or recommendations. A summary statement of the group decision about the problem.
- Reference list.

Appropriate citation method is that found in the *Journal of the American Dietetic Association*. See the January issue of the current year. Some examples follow:

Article

Quinn L, Leung P. Cost comparison of nutrient standard menus. *Journal of Nutrition & Menu Development.* 1996; 2: 49-71.

Book

Payne-Palacio J, Theis M. *West and Wood's Introduction to Foodservice,* 8th edition. Upper Saddle River, NJ: Prentice-Hall, Inc.; 1997.

Newspaper

Gibson R, Kilman S. Tainted hamburger incident heats up debate over US inspection system. *Wall Street Journal.* February 12, 1993: B1.

The following format may be followed for on-line sources and personal communication such as interviews, letters, memos, and E-mail.

Personal Communication

Brown S. Nutrient-standard menu planning (i.e. general topic). Personal communication. April 25, 1997.

On-line Sources

Foodmaker, Inc. Jack in the Box. [On-line]. September 15, 1997. http://www.foodmaker.com

WORKSHEETS

Worksheet 2 Food Safety
Problems: The Toxic Hamburger
Aftermath of the Outbreak
Joe Boggs

Name _____

Payne-Palacio and Theis   Chapter 3, Food Safety
Spears   Chapter 5, Food Safety (pg.131-154)

1.   Define and provide an example of the following hazards.
      a.   Chemical

      b.   Physical

      c.   Biological

2.   Explain three environmental conditions which contribute to the growth of bacteria.

      a.

      b.

      c.

3.   Identify three ways that foodborne illness may be transmitted from an infected person to food and back again to people.
      a.

      b.

      c.

13

4. Differentiate between two major types of foodborne illness (FBI).
    Foodborne infection

    Foodborne intoxication

    Identify a microorganism which causes an infection and produces a toxin.

5. Describe two examples of each type of FBI discussing foods implicated, symptoms, and ways to prevent an outbreak.

	Foods implicated	Symptoms	Prevention
Foodborne infection			
a.			
b.			

	Foods implicated	Symptoms	Prevention
Food borne intoxication			
a.			
b.			

6. Interpret how the control of time and temperature can be used to reduce the incidence of FBI.

7. Propose three appropriate cooling methods or guidelines to prevent FBI.
    a.

    b.

    c.

8.   Define cross-contamination.

9.   Describe at least five food handling practices wh   an be used to assure food
      safety.

      a.

      b.

      c.

      d.

      e.

10.   Define HACCP.

11.   Identify two foods which are potentially hazardous.
      a.

      b.

      For one of these food items create an HACCP flowchart   entify the five critical
      control points in a conventional foodservice system.

12.   Discuss the following agencies and their role in maintaining a safe food supply:

PHS:

FDA:

CDC:

EPA:

USDA:

13.   List two associations which provide unofficial food safety controls and standards to the foodservice industry.
a.

b.

14.   Interpret the role of the state and local agency (such as the Department of Health) in the regulation of food safety in the foodservice operation.

15.   Formulate an overview of the responsiblity of the foodservice manager in food safety.

Worksheet 3 Facility Maintenance
Problems: A System to Prevent Foodborne Illness
Joe Boggs
Ellen Jacobs

Name _____

Payne-Palacio and Theis   Chapter 8,   Cleaning, Sanitation, and Facility Safety
Spears   Chapter 5,   Food Safety (pg. 154-179.)
                                             Chapter 16, Sanitation and Maintenance of Equipment and Facilities

1.   Interpret the impact of layout and design of the foodservice organization on sanitation and maintenance.

2.   Differentiate between the terms cleaning and sanitation.

3.   List the two ways surfaces are sanitized effectively.
       a.

       b.

4.   For heat sanitization in a dishwasher, indicate the final rinse temperature required for conveyor or dual temperature machines.

5.   List the three common types of chemical sanitizers used in foodservice.
       a.

       b.

       c.

6. State the minimum number of sinks needed for manual pot and pan washing. Defend your answer.

7. Describe the controls for safety which should be built into warewashing (both manual and mechnical).

8. Discuss the factors to be considered when deciding between high temperature or chemical dishwashing machine systems.

9. State the maximum upper limit for heat sanitation. Discuss the effect that higher temperatures have on effective sanitation.

10. Prepare at least three major components to be utilized by management in a cleaning and maintenance program.
    a.

    b.

    c.

11. Define preventive maintenance. Assess how and why management should set up a preventive maintenance program.

12. Create an outline of a plan to be used to control rodents and insects in the foodservice operation.

13. Define and discuss the role of OSHA.

14. Describe the most common type of accidents sustained on the job in foodservice.

15. Identify the main components of a safety program which should be included to reduce and eliminate accidents.

16. Define the three classes of fire.
    a.

    b.

    c.

17. Design the components which should be included in an employee fire safety program.

Name _____

Payne-Palacio and Theis   Chapter 5, Purchasing, Receiving, and Storage
Spears   Chapter 8, Purchasing
     Chapter 9, Receiving, Storage, and Inventory Control

1.   Define the following terms:
Market

    Wholesaler

    Broker

    Retailer

    Brands (packer)

    Purchase Order

    Requisition

    Invoice

2.   Construct one example for each of the following which describes the effect each of these events has on purchasing in foodservice.
Economic

    Political

    Environmental

    Social

3.   Discuss one advantage and one disadvantage of bypassing individual marketing agents in the marketing channel.

4. Briefly describe the function of each of the following regulatory agencies.
   USDA

   FDA

   National Marine and Fisheries Service

5. Describe three characteristics the buyer should possess.
   a.

   b.

   c.

6. Define centralized and state one advantage.

   Infer what decentralized purchasing involves.

7. Define group purchasing and state and advantage.

   Indicate one possible disadvantage of this type of purchasing.

8. Differentiate between the following types of purchasing and discuss an advantage and disadvantage of each:

	Definition	Advantage	Disadvantage
Informal			
Formal			

9. State the type of foodservice organization likely to use informal purchasing.

   State the type of foodservice organization likely to use group purchasing.

10. List three alternative methods of purchasing and briefly discuss each.

   a.

   b.

   c.

11. Define Just-in-time purchasing (JIT) and briefly discuss its advantages.

12. What information would you need to evaluate the choice of making or buying dinner and sandwich rolls? What calculations would you make?

	MAKE	BUY
Information needed		
Calculations		

13. Differentiate between grading and inspecting meat.

14. Define specifications.

List information to be included in a specification.

a.

b.

c.

d.

e.

15. Some authorities recommend, "Level of quality purchased should match the intended use." State whether you agree or disagree with this recommendation and briefly defend your reasoning.

16. Define the following terms:

Receiving

Storage

Inventory

Inventory control

Mini-max method

FIFO

17. Briefly describe the characteristics expected of the individual responsible for receiving.

18.   Describe the equipment necessary to fulfill the receiving activity.

19.   List the steps the receiver should follow to accept and store the weekly dry goods order.
       a.

       b.

       c.

       d.

       e.

20.   Differentiate between the following:
       Blind receiving

       Invoice receiving

       In what instance(s) would blind receiving be suggested?

21.   List five characteristics the buyer can use to evaluate the vendor.
       a.

       b.

       c.

       d.

       e.

22. Identify at least three requirements for dry storage areas.
    a.

    b.

    c.

23. Explain at least three requirements for refrigerated and freezer storage.
    a.

    b.

    c.

24. Illustrate at least four sanitation practices to be implemented in the receiving and storage process.
    a.

    b.

    c.

    d.

25. Differentiate between a direct issue and a storeroom issue.

26. Compare and contrast physical and perpetual inventory.

27. Assess the purpose of the storeroom requisition and interpret its importance to inventory control.

28. Discuss why an overabundance of inventory on hand can be costly to the foodservice organization.

29. Describe how a well-planned receiving program contributes to cost and quality control.

30. Identify some potential consequences of a poorly planned and maintained receiving process.

Worksheet 7 Managing Food Production
Problems: Hilda Greene
June Jackson's Request
Ray Kroc
Henry Carnish
Janice Henley
Roast Beef Run-out

Name_____

Payne-Palacio and Theis	Chapter 6, Production Management
	Appendix A, Principles of Cooking
	Appendix B, Foodservice Equipment
Spears	Chapter 10, Production Planning
	Chapter 11, Ingredient Control
	Chapter 12, Quantity Food Production and Quality Control

1. Differentiate between quantity and quality in food production.

2. Discuss the impact the type of foodservice (conventional, commissary, ready-prepared, and assembly/serve) has on the production function of a foodservice operation.

3. List at least three advantages of standardized recipes.
    a.

    b.

    c.

4. Discuss why recipes must be standardized by a given foodservice organization and how this process is carried out.
    Why

    How

5. Describe how the format of a quantity food production recipe differs from a home style recipe.

6. Develop a written quality standard for the following products:
   Blueberry muffin

   Chicken salad

7. Adjust the following recipe to 235 portions using the percentage method.

   Beef Vegetable Soup
   Yield: 50 portions or 3 gal.   Portion: 1 cup (8 oz.)

Ingredients	Amount	Amount
Ground beef	8 lb. AP	
Onions, chopped	1 lb.	
Margarine	9 oz.	
Flour, all-purpose	9 oz.	
Beef stock	1 1/4 gal.	
Salt	1 Tbsp.	
Pepper, black	½ tsp.	
Carrots, fresh, diced	12 oz.	
Celery, sliced	10 oz.	
Mixed vegetables, frozen	4 lb.	
Tomatoes, diced, canned	2 lb. 8 oz.	

8. Adjust the following recipe to 110 portions using the factor method.

Chocolate Pudding
Yield: 50 portions or 6 qt.   Portion: ½ cup

Ingredient	Amount	Amount
Sugar, granulated	2 lb. 6 oz.	
Flour, all-purpose	6 oz.	
Cornstarch	3 oz.	
Salt	1 tsp.	
Cocoa	8 oz.	
Milk	1 gal.	
Margarine	8 oz.	
Vanilla	2 Tbsp.	

9. Define forecasting.

10. Discuss the costs associated with overproduction.

   Discuss the costs associated with underproduction.

11. List examples of the type of data to be collected for historical records in the following types of foodservice operations.
   Full service restaurant

   Limited service restaurant

   School lunch program

   Hospital operating both patient foodservice and a cafeteria

12. Using moving average of three days predict the number of meals which should be prepared for the next Monday.

DAY	WEEK 1	WEEK 2	WEEK 3	WEEK 4
Monday	360	375	367	373
Tuesday	372	381	376	380
Wednesday	375	373	378	376
Thursday	358	368	360	363
Friday	333	377	353	370

13. Calculate the number of pounds of ground beef required to make a 4 ounce cooked beef patty for 640 people at an 80% yield.

14. Discuss why the production schedule should include information on the amount of leftovers and substitutions for run outs. State how this information can be used.

Discuss other categories of information to be included on the production sheet.

15. Describe the activities that occur in an ingredient room.

16. List at least three advantages of an ingredient room
    a.

    b.

    c.

17. Assess why portion control is essential in quantity foodservice.

18. Illustrate three ways to assure portion control.
    a.

    b.

    c.

19. If you portioned chocolate pudding with a #10 scoop, how many portions could you expect to get from 3 quarts of pudding? (Show all calculations)

20. Discuss how portion control relates to recipe standardization.

21. Discuss the relationship between the purchasing and production functions in foodservice.

22. List the major reasons for cooking food.
    a.

    b.

    c.

23. List and describe three methods by which heat can be transferred.
    a.

    b.

    c.

24. Define the moist heat method of cooking.

25. Describe three pieces of equipment which can be used with this method.
    a.

    b.

    c.

26. Differentiate between the following:
    Simmer

    Stew

    Poach

    Blanch

    Braise

    Steam

    Roast

27. Discriminate between the following cooking methods:
Broil

Grill

Griddle

Pan broil

28. Explain the difference between the following cooking methods:
Deep fry

Pan fry

Sauté

29. Vegetables can be cooking in a steam jacketed kettle, although this is not the preferred piece of equipment. Discuss why this is so and what piece(s) of equipment optimally cook vegetables.

30. Describe the differences between the following ovens:
Deck

Convection

Rotary

Combination

Impingement

Cook and hold

Worksheet 9 Financial Management and Cost Control
Problems: Jeff Jordan

Name _____

Payne-Palacio and Theis   Chapter 16, Financial Management (pages 493-519)
Spears   Chapter 21,Management of Financial Resources

1.   Discuss and briefly describe three requirements of a recordkeeping system.
      a.

      b.

      c.

2.   Calculate the food cost percentage for the day if food cost is $1030/day and
      income is $2550. Show all calculations.

3.   Explain why daily variances in food cost are not cause for concern, but deviations
      over several months would be.

4.   What is the purpose of the Profit and Loss statement (P&L)?

5.   List two examples of potential revenue in a school food program.
      a.

      b.

      In a hospital
      a.

      b.

6. Calculate the cost of food sold (sales) for the month of November. Show all calculations.

Purchases in November	$10,500
November 30 Inventory	$2,250
October 31 Inventory	$1,950

7. For the above problem, calculate percent food cost of sales if income is $25,000. Show all calculations.

8. Calculate the labor cost percentage if labor expense is $32,000 and revenue equals $62,000. Show all calculations.

9. Define controllable expenses and give two examples.

10. Define the break even point (BEP).

11. Calculate the BEP for the following operation. Show all calculations.

Fixed cost	$14,000
Variable Cost	$30,000
Sales	$50,000

12. State two examples of fixed costs.
    a.

    b.

13. State two examples of variable costs.
    a.

    b.

14. List three ratios used to analyze costs.
    a.

    b.

    c.

15. Predict how you would use a labor ratio to justify a change in food production method.

16. Interpret management's responsiblity in financial control through an awareness of "where the money is going before it is gone."

PROBLEMS

JOAN THOMKINS
Worksheet 1 Scope of the Foodservice Industry

Joan Thomkins is a school foodservice supervisor of a suburban school district. She has been employed by the school lunch program for over 18 years and has always enjoyed the job.

In early September the school guidance counselor, Hazel Smith, dropped by Joan's office and asked her to participate in a round table discussion about careers in foodservice for interested high school students at the end of the month. She said there would be a panel discussion including a human resources representative from Tricon Global Restaurants, Marriott-Sodexho Company and a military recruiter who would discuss opportunities in foodservice management in the military services.

Hazel said, "Joan, I'd like you to talk to the students about careers in foodserivce. I've asked all of our guests to do the same from their perspective. From what I understood from Tricon, they run three businesses, including KFC. Marriott-Sodexho has a lot of different types of business interests, and Major Jones, the Army recruiter, will talk about the Quartermaster Corps and other places where military folks serve food. He is going to bring some of those fancy meal packs that they use in the field. I think they are called MREs and the students will get to taste them. What I thought you could do is discuss jobs in school lunch. Talk about the required education and training needed, salaries, what you like about your job. You know what I mean."

Joan thought about it and was ready to agree when Hazel said, "Oh by the way. Are there any other places that people with your background work? It might be useful to mention these to let the students know about other opportunities." Joan agreed that there were many other opportunities and said she would be willing to put something together.

A week before the session Joan was beginning to regret that she agreed to make this ten minute talk. She began making a list of the types of organizations that have foodservice operations. It occurred to her that although her school district was self-operated, there were some programs managed by contractors. She had no experience with this type of business but thought the students should hear about these opportunities as well.

1. **Develop a visual aid that Joan can use to provide an overview of the foodservice industry.**
2. **How do Sodexho-Marriott, Tricon, the military, and school foodservice fit into this overview?**

THE TOXIC HAMBURGER[1]
Worksheet 2 Food Safety

In May of 1992 Bremerton-Kitsap County Health Department i
Washington sent a bulletin to all of the operators of foodserv
identifying new standards for the production of hamburgers. The bulletin was ...
a change in Washington State Health Policy in March of 1992 which was widely publicizea.
A major requirement was that hamburgers be cooked to an internal temperature of 155
degrees F.[2]

In early January of 1993 a large number of cases of foodborne illness (FBI) were
diagnosed in and around Washington State. By January 15th there were over 150 people
sick, most of them children and one child had already died. What most of the sick people
had in common was that they had eaten hamburgers obtained from Jack in the Box
restaurants. The final total number of laboratory confirmed cases was 583 although 708
people were reported to have become ill. Symptoms of the disease occurred four to nine
days after eating the hamburgers and included bloody diarrhea and cramps. A few young
children developed complications including HUS. Not all of those who became ill actually
ate the hamburgers.

In 1993 Foodmaker, Inc. was the operator of two concepts, Jack in the Box
restaurants and Chi-Chi's restaurants. Foodmaker had 55 company owned and 10
franchised Jack in the Box restaurants in Washington State. Initially executives of the
corporation which is located in San Diego, California indicated they had not received notice
of the higher temperature requirement. Chuck Duddles, executive vice president and chief
financial officer of Foodmaker indicated, "We are not expected to be experts on disease.
We have to depend on the experts at the Department of Agriculture to set the standards.
We are not a research firm."[1] Operating procedures in Jack in the Box stores required that
hamburgers be cooked to an internal temperature of 140 degrees F which was the
recommended temperature by the USDA in 1993.[3]

1.   What was the most likely cause of this outbreak?
2.   Do you feel that Foodmaker was or was not liable for the foodborne illness? Justify
        your answer.

---

[1]HoldenBA. State says chain involved in outbreak didn't comply with new cooking rule. *Wall Street J,*
Jan. 25, 1993.

[2]Holden BA. Foodmaker delays expansion plans in wake of food poisioning outbreak.*Wall Street J,*
Feb. 16, 1993.

[3]Gibson R, Kilman S. Tainted hamburger incident heats up debate over U.S. meat inspection system.
Wall Street J, Feb 12, 1993.

A SYSTEM TO PREVENT FOODBORNE ILLN/
Worksheet 3 Facility Maintenance

On hearing the news of the *outbreak* of foodborne disease restaurants increased the cooking time from 2 minutes minutes and 15 seconds. They also turned the burger one additiona. ...

The company hoped to recover over $300 million in damages from Vons Cos, Inc. their meat supplier, in spite of acknowledging that Vons was not required to test the meat for microorganisms. Additionally there were USDA inspectors on site in the meat plant. Foodmaker also acknowledged that they did not adhere to the higher internal temperature standard. Jack Goodall, president of Foodmaker, however, said, "We don't thinking cooking is the issue. What happened here is we received some terribly poisoned meat that we never should have received."[1]

Foodmaker rolled out a complete restaurant HACCP system. They hired a food safety expert, Dr. David Theno, to lead the quality assurance and product safety division. His first assignment was to look at the suppliers and get rid of those who may have provided contaminated products. He sampled products and tested for contamination[2].

Develop a recipe for hamburgers including HACCP requirements.

---

[1]Martin R. Foodmaker's Goodall eyes two turnabouts from Family deal. *Nation's Restaurant News* 1994; 28(13): 7,151.

[2]Anon. Foodmaker, Food Lion work to restore image. *Food Protection Report* June, 1994.

AFTERMATH OF THE *OUTBREAK*
Worksheet 2 Food Safety

Foodmaker, Inc. was a firm which had been in operation for 43 years. At the start of 1993 it operated two types of restaurants; 1,155 Jack in the Box operations in the western and southwestern US, Hong Kong, and Mexico, and 231 Chi-Chi's. (Table I)

In March of 1992 Foodmaker, Inc. completed an initial public offering (IPO) of 17,151,000 shares of common stock. The price of the stock declined after the *outbreak*. Trading in Foodmaker stock was halted on Friday, January 22, 1993 when news of the *outbreak* of foodborne disease started spreading. The stock price plummeted 32% from $13.875 on January 15th to $9.50 when trading was halted. It dropped $2.50 on January 22nd alone.[1] Foodmaker stock never paid a dividend because the firm wished to use earnings for growth in the firm. Earnings per share for the 12 month period ending March 1994 were -$1.22.[2] All together Foodmaker lost $98 million in 1993 due to bad press, accounting adjustments and post-retirement benefits. Half of the losses were due to the *outbreak*.[3]

The company provided a reduction of franchise rents and royalties of $3.8 million to franchise holders. In fiscal year 1992 the company earned $38.8 million from franchisees and in 1993 received only $35.2 million.

Foodmaker chairman, Jack W. Goodall, Jr., reported to shareholders in February 1993 that the company intended to defer all capital expenditures which meant delaying plans to open 85 new stores that year.[4] At that time the company reported that lawsuits had been filed against the company. Foodmaker was itself suing the meat supplier, Vons Cos. of Arcadia, California for losses as a result of the *outbreak*.

The company believed that their insurance of $100 million was adequate to cover the lawsuits related to the *outbreak*. Ultimately the company covered medical expenses for all victims: established a $450,000 medical monitoring and trust fund for victims[5] as a result of a class action lawsuit brought by victims and their families; and settled up to $1.3

---

[1]Holden BA. State says chain involved in outbreak didn't comply with new cooking rule. *Wall Street J.* Jan. 21, 1993.

[2]Foodmaker 10-K report. Compact Disclosure

[3]Anon. Foodmaker loses $98 million in 1993. *Nation's Restaurant News* 1993; 27(46).

[4]Holden BA. Foodmaker delays expansion plans in wake of foodpoisoning outbreak. *Wall Street J.* Feb. 16, 1993.

[5]Anon. Foodmaker sets up trust fund for food poisoning victims. *Nation's Restaurant News* 1993; 27(47): 2.

million[1] for each of four wrongful death suits.

Other costs to the firm included an increase in advertising costs of $15 million. Advertising and promotion expenses in 1992 were $69.2 million and in 1993, $84.3 million.[2]

In February 1994 Family Restaurants, Inc. (formerly Restaurant Enterprises Group, Inc. which had been operating under Chapter 11 bankruptcy) agreed to buy Chi-Chi's's from Foodmaker. Foodmaker received about $200 million in cash plus 40% equity in Family Restaurants. The effect of this sale was that Foodmaker consisted of only Jack in the Box restaurants. Family Restaurants was composed of El Torito, Coco's, Carrows, Casa Gallardo and Chi-Chi's, all Mexican-style family restaurants. Jack Goodall became chairman and chief executive officer of both Foodmaker, Inc. and Family Restaurants, Inc.[3]

1. **How well has Foodmaker coped with the catastrophe?**
2. **What about Family Restaurants?**
3. **What other entities were affected by the *outbreak*? How did they react?**

[1]Anon. Foodmaker paying $1.3 M in last of 4 *E. coli* deaths. *Nation's Restaurant News* 1994;28(9):2.

[2]Foodmaker, Inc. Annual Report, 1994.

[3]REGI, now Family, buys Chi-Chi's to end reorganization. *Nation's Restaurant News* 1994; 28(6).

TABLE I: SELECTED FINANCIAL DATA FOR FOODMAKER, INC. (Source - Annual Report - Compustat PC Plus Corporate Text

(Dollars in millions, except per share data)	For the fiscal year ending Oct.3, 1993	For the fiscal year ending Sept.27,1992
JACK IN THE BOX restaurants	1,172	1,155
Company operated	725	720
Franchise operated	447	435
CHI-CHI'S Restaurants	235	232
Company operated	207	181
Franchise operated	28	51
JACK IN THE BOX comparable restaurant sales trend	(7.4%)	2.4%
CHI-CHI'S comparable restaurant sales trend	(5.2%)	(2.3%)
System wide sales	$1,459.2	$1,486.5
JACK IN THE BOX	1,026.1	1,043.7
CHI-CHI'S	433.1	444.8
Revenues	$1,240.7	$1,219.3
Earnings (loss) before interest and taxes (*)	$ (8.6)	$ 111.2
Earnings (loss) (*)	$ (44.1)	$ 21.9
Earnings (loss) per share (*)	$ (1.15)	$ .67
Net loss	$ (98.1)	$ (41.8)
Net loss per share	$ (2.55)	$ (1.28)
Cash provided by operations	$ 25.7	$ 66.7
Total assets	$ 890.4	$915.5
Total stockholders' equity	$ 139.1	$246.9
Book value per share	$ 3.64	$ 6.47
Common shares outstanding, in thousands	38,234	38,149

(*) Before extraordinary item and cumulative effect of changes in accounting principles.

Menu	Thursday	Friday
Breakfast	Grapefruit juice Orange sections Scrambled eggs Tst. english muffin Butter/Jelly Milk/Hot Chocolate	Orange juice Sliced cantaloupe French toast w/ syrup Milk/Hot Chocolate
Lunch	Chicken noodle soup Chicken salad sandwiches Apple slices Milk	Cream of tomato soup Grl. cheese sandwiches Sliced tomatoes and cucumbers Fresh strawberry shortcake Milk
Dinner	Sliced ham Au gratin potatoes Tossed salad/French dressing Cornbread/ butter Sliced peaches Milk	COOKOUT Grl hot dogs/hamburgers Baked beans Potato salad Celery & carrot sticks Watermelon "Samores" Sodas-Lemonade

ELLEN JACOBS
Worksheet 3 Facility Maintenance

Ellen Jacobs, R.D. is the nutrition care manager for a large nursing home. She is the employee of a contractor which was hired to manage the foodservice operation. There are three other contractor employees: the foodservice director (FSD) (Jay), assistant manager (Bruce), assistant manager for the three outer buildings (Jennifer), and the purchaser (Chris). This management team has been in place for six months after their company won the contract away from another management company which had the contract for over six years.

The facility is a 900 bed skilled care facility. The main building houses 450 residents on 12 floors. There are 38 residents on each floor. There are three smaller intermediate care units, two of which have dining rooms where residents eat together.

Ellen, among her other duties, is responsible for scheduling the supervisors and diet technicians. In addition she has been assigned the responsibility for training. Ellen usually schedules for one month at a time. She asks that the supervisors and techs submit requests for vacations and other time off three months ahead. Managers, except the FSD, are on call every third weekend. Techs are able to cover for supervisors but supervisors are not trained to handle the technician role.

On May 15th Ellen was planning the schedule for June. Grace had requested the first two weeks for vacation; Carl wanted weeks 2 and 3; Jerri wanted the fourth week off to get ready for her wedding which was planned for June 27th.

It is desirable to have an early and late supervisor in both the main building and the outer buildings each day. Two early techs and at least one late tech are needed. Hours for supervisors and techs are 6-1:30 or 11:30-7:30. Training for techs occurs each Wednesday so it is helpful if all are scheduled that day.

On May 13th one of the supervisors (Dorothy) had been injured on the job. She retrieved a box which was on a high shelf in the store room. She used an office chair with wheels to climb up. As she was reaching for the box, the chair rolled out from under her, causing her to fall. Ellen learned that Dorothy had broken her coccyx and would not be able to return to work for six weeks.

1. **Develop a schedule for supervisors and technicians.**
2. **Evaluate the safety standards for the organization.**

Schedule for supervisors and technicians
May 30-June 27

Ma 30-Jn 13	S	M	T	W	TH	F	S	S	M	T	W	TH	F	S
Supervisors														
Angela (Main)														
Betty (Main)														
Carl (Outer)														
Dorothy (Outer)														
Evelyn (Outer)														
Technicians														
Florence (Main)														
Grace (Main)														
Hal (Main)														
Jerri (Outer)														
Karen (Outer)														

June 14-27	S	M	T	W	TH	F	S	S	M	T	W	TH	F	S
Supervisors														
Angela (Main)														
Betty (Main)														
Carl (Outer)														
Dorothy (Outer)														
Evelyn (Outer)														
Technicians														
Florence (Main)														
Grace (Main)														
Hal (Main)														
Jerri (Outer)														
Karen (Outer)														

THOMAS JEFFERSON ELEMENTARY SCHOOL
Worksheet 4 The Menu

Each year Irene Maiwald, the supervisor of foodservices for the Pleasant Valley School District, surveys one age group for overall satisfaction with the school lunch program. This year in the Spring she looked at the upper level elementary schools grades 4 through 6 which included Thomas Jefferson. (See student profile in Table 1.)

Satisfaction surveys were completed by students and faculty at the three schools serving fourth through sixth grades. Generally the students thought the food was O.K. They felt they got enough to eat and there was always peanut butter and jelly if they didn't like the hot meal on the line. Some of the surveys indicated that the people who had early lunch had hotter food that was of better quality than the students who had third lunch. (See meal hours in Table 2.) Comments such as, "Food is dried out," "Vegetables are very yucky," "Hamburgers taste like hockey pucks," "What is this mystery meat?" and "Why can't we have McDonald's Happy Meals or Pizza Hut?" were more frequent from the students who had the last lunch. One of the suggestions from the student surveys was to add sandwiches as a choice.

Pleasant Valley School District is a suburban district, very close to a city of 350,000 people. The district has a large proportion of middle class residents, most of whom own their own homes. The median price for a home is $175,000. There is a substantial population of poor families in the district as well. About one fifth of the students come from families which are considered to have earnings near the poverty line. The ethnic background is mixed as well. The students are predominately Caucasian but there is an increasing population of students of African American background (15%) many of whose families are employed by the chemical and banking industries. There is a small but increasing population of Latino students most of whom are relatively poor.

Irene creates a menu each month for the schools under her supervision. Generally many of the same foods are used but not always in the same order or with the same accompaniments. Irene is feeling considerable pressure to modify the menu in some way. Students who have grown up with quick service restaurants want to have more fast food type items.

School administrators are very concerned with keeping the costs of the meal low. They have also indicated that beginning in January they intend to put meters into each of the school cafeterias and charge Irene for the electricity, water and gas used in each operation.

Of late there have been increasingly confrontational news reports about the unhealthy foods available in school lunch programs. Even the U.S. Department of Agriculture reported that school meals were too high in fat, sodium and saturated fat. Then USDA Secretary Mike Espy commented, "So the news is simple: We can't continue to deep fry our children's health.[1] The most recent regulation "School Meals Initiative for Healthy Children" required implementation of the 1990 Dietary Guidelines for Americans. Programs may plan menus based on NuMenus, Assisted NuMenus, or food-based.

Parents have called Irene to discuss the nutritional quality of the food. A recent call from a parent began, "I am concerned about the food offered at Thomas Jefferson Elementary School. In the last three days lunch included chicken nuggets and french fries, hot dogs, and pizza. My husband's family has a history of coronary artery disease and my son who is in 4th grade already has high blood cholesterol. If I knew in advance what was going to be served I would pack a lunch for Robert to be certain he wouldn't eat these bad foods. I feel your menu is not healthy and you should do something about it. Don't you care about the future health of your students?"

As Irene hangs up the phone, she thinks to herself, "Of course I care about my children's health. But their favorite foods are high in fat. Do I need to cut out all fast foods or maybe even all fat from the menu?" Irene further speculates about the three options for planning menus. Mulling this over she thinks, "Maybe I should begin using NuMenus. Possibly a computer will answer all of my questions."

Irene has been trying to encourage students to consume school lunch meals. Much of the literature suggests that students who eat these meals are better nourished than students who bring their lunch or who purchase meals from off-grounds locations. Around 80% of the potential customers do eat the school lunch. Irene has made available pre-paid meals so that meal tickets may be purchased in advance. In the sixth grade a number of the boys buy two or three lunches each day using pre-paid meal tickets because they are so hungry.

Each year Irene receives a list of the types of commodity foods which will be available for the next year through the surplus foods program. The formula used to calculate her allocations are $.145 for each meal served the previous year to be used only to purchase commodities. (See list of available commodities, Table 3.)   She also can have access to bonus foods which she can get, if available, at no cost. She fills most of her purchasing requirements on the open market, however.

All schools have kitchens where the food is produced. Kitchens are provided with similar equipment (Table 4).

As Irene plans the menu she begins to wonder where to begin and if she can satisfy anybody.

1.   **What is the National School Lunch Program?**
2.   **Plan one week of the menu for October using a food-based menu planning process.**
       (Use menu planning assignment form, pg. 113.)

---

[1]USDA says: 'We can't continue to deep fry our children's health'. *Food Management*. 1993;28(12)

3. Plan the second week of the menu for October using NuMenus or Assisted NuMenus menu planning. Incorporate the following into the required nutrient standards averaged over a five day period. (Use menu planning assignment form, pg.114.)
    - Calories - plus or minus 5% of target
    - Fat - no more than 30% of calories from fat
    - Saturated fat - no more than 10% of calories from saturated fat
    - Protein - maximum of 20 grams
    - Iron - plus or minus 10% of target

4. Write a one page analysis and justification of which menu planning system you suggest that Irene utilize.

Table 1:   Students in Pleasant Valley School District

Schools	Number	Grades	Students per school	Total Students	% eating lunch
High School - Ray Kroc	1	9-12	1100	1100	75
Middle Schools	2	7-8	300	600	45
Upper Elementary	3	4-6	300	900	80
Lower Elementary	5	k-3	240	1200	80

Table 2:   Meal Hours

Lunch Period	Hours
First Lunch	11:15-11:45
Second Lunch	11:55-12:25
Third Lunch	12:30-1:00

Table 3: Expected Commodity List For the 1999 School Year (USDA Food & Consumer Svc.Office)

Beans, green, cnd 6/10	Apple Juice 12/46 oz	Chicken, frz cut-up 40#
Beans, vegetarian 6/10	Orange Juice, frz. conc.	Chicken, frz breaded 30#
Carrots, frozen, 40#	Apples, fresh 40#	Chicken, frz. cooked,diced
Corn, liquid 6/10	Apple Slices, cnd 6/10	Turkey, frz, whole 40#
Corn, frozen 30#	Applesauce, cnd 6/10	Turkey roasts, frz 4/8-12#
Peas, green frozen 30#	Grapefruit, fresh, 34-39#	Turkey, frz, ground 4/10#
Potato wedges, 6/5#	Oranges, fresh, 34-39#	Eggs, frz, whole, 6/5#
Potato rounds, frz 6/5#	Apricots, frozen 20#	Beef roasts, round 40#
Potato, oven fry 6/5#	Apricots, cnd 6/10	Beef, frz, ground 36#
Potato, russet, fresh, 50#	Cherries, red 6/10	Beef patties, extra lean 36#
Sweet Potato, mashed 6/10	Cherries, frozen 30#	Pork, frz, ground 36#
Spaghetti Sauce, 40#	Blueberries, wild, frz 30#	Ham, water, cooked 40#
Tomato Paste	Blueberries, cult, frz 30#	Pork Ham Roast, frz 40#
	Peaches, cling, sliced 6/10	Pork, Sausage Patties 1.5
	Peaches, diced 6/10	oz
	Peaches, frozen, 20#	Cheese, cheddar low fat
	Pears, sliced cnd 6/10	40#
	Pears, diced cnd 6/10	Cheese, process sliced 6/5#
	Pineapple chunks 6/10	Cheese, mozzarella 48#
	Mixed Fruit, cnd 6/10	Cheese, mozzarella lite 48#
	Prunes, pitted 25#	Cheese, american/skim
	Raisins, 48/1#	blend
		Milk, NFD 50#
Flour, AP 4/10#	Rice, milled, long grain 25#	*Note: This list is an*
Flour, bread 5/10#	Oil, reduced fat 6/1 Gals	*estimate. The availability of*
Macaroni 20# ctn	Oil, vegetable 6/1 Gals	*these commodities depends*
Macaroni, rotini, 20# ctn	Shortening, vegetable 12/3	*on market conditions. In*
Oats, rolled 12/3	Spaghetti, enriched 20# ctn	*addition, other commodities*
Peanut Butter, cnd 6/10		*may become available*
Peanut Butter, reduced fat		*during the year.*
Peanuts roasted, cnd 6/10		*Source: USDA Food &*
		Consumer Service Office

Table 4:   Kitchen Equipment Available

Restaurant style range	Meat slicer
One 40 gallon SJK	Reach in freezer
Griddle	Two reach in refrigerators
Deep Fat Fryer	Cafeteria line with three well hot food
Four convection ovens	compartment
Compartment steamer	

PLEASANT VALLEY SCHOOL DISTRICT FOODSERVICE
Worksheet 5 Purchasing, Receiving, and Inventory Control

Each year in June Irene Maiwald, supervisor of foodservices for the school district, prepares Requests for Bid for the next year. She does this after she has received information about what commodity foods will be available the next year and after she has developed the menu based on survey results of the previous year. This is a task that she does not enjoy very much. First she has to determine how much of each product group she will need for the next year. She needs to know how many students she will be serving during the next year to help her determine how much food to order. (See students in Pleasant Valley School District. Table 1) She must identify vendors willing and able to bid for her business.

Irene has been thinking about ways to increase the amount of fresh fruit and fresh vegetables on the menu. She planned to call several vendors each week to get quotations on the fruit and vegetables to be used the next week. Irene developed specifications for most of the canned, chilled, and frozen products served but not for the new fresh fruits and vegetables she would like to include.

Irene has received information at a recent trade show about foods that have been engineered to have lower fat content. Since hot dogs are popular with students in all grades and she wants to include sandwiches in the menu, she wants to explore both hot dogs and deli meats/cheeses to find out which would be acceptable in terms of taste, nutritional quality, and cost.

As she was working through developing the Requests for Bid she received a phone call from Jennifer Hargrove, the foodservice supervisor in a nearby school district. Jennifer and Irene know each other well after being involved in many of the same professional organizations and working on some committees together. Jennifer was very excited about an idea she had and wanted to try it out on Irene. "I have just been thinking about the problem with food costs. Commodity foods are uncertain at best, and sometimes we don't get all that we need. This means we have to go into the market to get materials which raises food costs. I don't know how you are surviving, but I am having real difficulty coming in under budget, especially since labor costs are increasing. I wondered if we could get a better price if we bought food and supplies together. I believe the distributors would reduce the cost per unit if we were buying more units. I am buying for 14 schools with a total enrollment of about 5000 students. You have how many?"

Irene responded, "I have 11 schools and about 3800 students."

Jennifer said, "Right. Now how much more important would we be with almost 9000 students per day compared with going into the market separately?"

Irene thought, "While you've been talking I just thought that we could involve several more school districts, not just our two. This could be really big! I can see some great opportunities, but there also could be some problems."

1. **Should Irene and Jennifer combine to purchase food and supplies?**
2. **Develop specifications for a fresh fruit, vegetable, and hot dog for the School Lunch Program.**

Table 1:   **Students in Pleasant Valley School District**

Schools	Number	Grades	Students per school	Total Students	% eating lunch
High School - Ray Kroc	1	9-12	1100	1100	75
Middle Schools	2	7-8	300	600	45
Upper Elementary	3	4-6	300	900	80
Lower Elementary	5	k-3	240	1200	80

IRENE'S LONG TERM PLAN
Worksheet 6   Food Production Methods

All of the schools in the Pleasant Valley School District have production and service at each school. The lunch items are made each day and served on a straight line cafeteria. Sometimes cooking is done in advance on items such as turkeys or puddings to be served the next day.

The menu for K-3 includes the hot meal or peanut butter and jelly sandwiches. For grades 4-6 the menu is the same with the addition of a sandwich choice. Grades 7-8 have of choice of two hot entrees or a packaged salad (chicken, chef's or tuna). High school students have a choice of two hot entree, deli bar or salad bar.

Each school has an on-site cook/manager who works 7 hours per day. The high school has three additional cooks (5 hours each), two cold preparation positions (5 hours each), plus three positions (4 hours each) for serving and clean up (ware washing). All of the other schools run with a cook/manager and one additional cook, two cold prep. positions and two service positions.

The kitchens are fully equipped but several need to be updated. As Irene Maiwald, supervisor of foodservices for the school district, looks around she observes that five of the eleven schools have equipment which dates from the 1960s when the schools were built. The maintenance cost on old equipment is increasing. In some cases, parts are no longer available so Irene needs to consider replacing some or all of the equipment in many units.

The income that Irene receives comes from three sources. Cash register receipts, Federal Government funding, and State funding to support salaries. Cash register receipts and Federal funding are based on the actual meals served. (See Per meal income. Table 1) Currently 20% of students receive free meals and 5% reduced price meals. (See Table 2 for number of students enrolled in each school.) Irene can also sell a'la carte items which are not counted as part of the National School Lunch Program (NSLP) and for which no federal monies can be reimbursed. These items include juices, crackers, ice cream, and milk. On a daily basis about $250.00 is received from a'la carte sales. State money to support salaries is $1.35 for each hour worked. (See wages paid for each labor position. Table 3)

As Irene looks at her budget it is apparent she is spending much of her income for labor. The amount she spends is clearly too high, especially since she will soon have to pay for utilities from her income. She needs to develop a method to reduce total labor costs while maintaining quality foodservice in all eleven schools.

Develop a plan for Irene.

Table 1: **Per Meal Income**

Type of meal	Money from students	Money from Federal Government
Paid	$ .90	$ .17
Reduced price	.40	.97
Free	0	1.97

Table 2: **Students in Pleasant Valley School District**

Schools	Number	Grades	Students per school	Total Students	% eating lunch
High School - Ray Kroc	1	9-12	1100	1100	75
Middle Schools	2	7-8	300	600	45
Upper Elementary	3	4-6	300	900	80
Lower Elementary	5	k-3	240	1200	80

Table 3: **Wages and Benefits Paid**

Position	Rate per hour
Cook/manager	$ 9.50
Cook	7.50
Cold preparation	6.50
Service	6.00

HILDA GREENE

Irene Maiwald, the supervisor of foodservices for the Pleasant Valley School District, made it a point to try to get to a different school each week and to have lunch with the students. She observed production, watched the cafeteria line as students selected their foods, and sampled all foods. In most of the schools the food seemed pretty good to her and met quality standards.

When Irene took the temperature of the food on the line she found that temperatures were within standards for the most part. (See record of food temperatures. Table 1) All schools were required to maintain logs of food temperatures. Cook/managers were to record the temperature of the food when it was finished cooking and when it was placed in the hot food table or the chilled section of the cafeteria line. Irene was concerned about the temperature of the food served at Thomas Jefferson. She made an effort to speak with the cook/manager of that site. Hilda Greene was a cook who had been with the school lunch program for many years. She considered the kitchen her domain and she was definitely "in charge." Hilda loved the students and they reciprocated her affection. They called her "Mamma Hilda" and she knew each of them by name. She also knew all of their older siblings and would ask about them.

When Irene asked Hilda about the temperatures, initially Hilda indicated she was too busy to discuss it right then. Irene suggested they meet at 1:30 and asked that Hilda bring the temperature log with her. She also asked to see the recipes Hilda was using for both the macaroni and cheese and the spaghetti sauce. Although both products were good, they didn't taste like the products served in other schools. The spaghetti sauce seemed a little bland. The macaroni and cheese was very rich and creamy, quite yummy. In addition the green beans were soft and olive gray in color.

The temperature logs indicated that when the macaroni and cheese came out of the oven it was 185° F but when it was placed in the hot food table the temperature had dropped to 160° F. Likewise the temperature of the spaghetti sauce when removed from the SJK was 180° F but was only 140° F when it reached the cafeteria line. Hilda commented, "My kids really don't like to burn their mouths and you know how hot macaroni and cheese can get."

When Irene asked about the use of recipes, Hilda was at first reluctant to discuss them. She pointed out that the recipes were those provided by the school district. She said, "My children just love both the mac & cheese and my spaghetti. They all say it is better than what they have at home. I can't see why you are upset about this." Irene noticed that the recipes were perfectly clean, just as they left the school district office.

Irene indicated she was not upset. "I am curious about why your products are so different from those we serve elsewhere. I would really like to understand the difference."

Hilda could not provide a good answer so Irene decided to return the next time the products were made. When spaghetti was next served she discovered that Hilda did not use any onions, pepper, or Worcestershire sauce for the product. She indicated that her kids did not like spicy foods. On mac & cheese day Irene found that for 200 portions, Hilda used 22 pounds of sharp cheddar cheese and four pounds of margarine.

1. Calculate the impact of Hilda's changes to the recipes on food cost and nutritional composition. (See Food Prices, Table 2)
2. What if anything should Irene do about food production at Thomas Jefferson School?

Table 1:   **Record of Food Temperatures** - Degrees Fahrenheit

HAGGERTY ELEMENTARY		BENJ FRANKLIN ELEMENTARY		THOMAS JEFFERSON	
Spaghetti sauce	155	Hot dogs	142	Macaroni & cheese	120
Spaghetti noodles	140	Baked beans	145	Stewed tomatoes	132
Green beans	148	Milk	42	Milk	40
Milk	41	Apple Brn Betty	50	Chocolate pudding	45
Fruit Cocktail	50				

HAGGERTY ELEMENTARY		BENJ FRANKLIN ELEMENTARY		THOMAS JEFFERSON	
Sliced turkey	138	Chicken nuggets	155	Spaghetti sauce	134
Gravy	145	French fries	160	Spaghetti noodles	125
Mashed Potatoes	142	Cole slaw	42	Green beans	110
Succotash	144	Milk	40	Milk	46
Milk	40	Applesauce	50	Fruit cocktail	44
Brownies	72				

Table 2:   **Food Prices**

Product	unit	price per unit
Macaroni noodles	2/5 lb	$ 5.94
Salt	1/25 lb	3.14
Vegetable oil	6/1 lb	24.35
Margarine	30/1 lb	16.17
All purpose flour	2/25 lb	10.00
Dry mustard	6/1 lb	17.06
Worcestershire sauce	4/1 Gal	16.89
Milk	4/1 Gal	7.76
Sharp cheddar cheese	1/10 lb	20.61
Bread crumbs	6/5 lb	18.21
Ground beef	3/10 lb	41.49
Tomato puree	6/10 lb	14.49
Tomato sauce	6/10 lb	12.99
Onions	1/15 lb	25.38
Bay leaves	3/10 oz	16.71
Thyme, ground	6/7 oz	21.86
Garlic	6/25 oz	26.13
Oregano, dried	3/1.5 lb	31.07
Basil, dried	6/5 oz	16.74
Sugar, granulated	1/25 lb	9.15
Cayenne pepper	6/1 lb	18.54
Spaghetti	2/10 lb	9.23

JANICE HENLEY
Worksheet 7 Managing Food Production

Janice Henley was director of retail operations for a large medical center. She supervised a cafeteria which served over 6000 customers daily. In addition she also supervised catering operations which included simple coffee service up to sit-down wait-served six course dinners for 400 people.

There were several signature items on the cafeteria menu which had been served for many years and which were very popular. Macaroni and Cheese was served with stewed tomatoes, both homemade from recipes used for a long time. The mac and cheese standardized recipe produced 48 portions (#8 dipper). Janice noticed that the production sheet called for 600 portions (factor 12.5). But the cash register receipts showed only 450 portions were sold. There was no Macaroni and Cheese left over. Janice checked and discovered that customers could order one portion (one dipper) or two portions (two dippers) and both of these could be entered into the register so that all portions sizes could be captured. The price for one portion was $1.25 which reflected a 28% food cost. Customers complained angrily to the servers if they received a level dipper of Macaroni and Cheese.

Another signature item was Shrimp Creole. The most recent time it was served customers complained because they only received two shrimps in each portion. When Janice checked she discovered that the cooks had used the shrimp which was usually used for Shrimp Cocktails in the recipe (Extra Jumbo, 16-20) instead of the extra large (26-35) shrimp usually used. Extra Jumbo cost $20.00 per pound (peeled and deveined). They are $3.00 less per pound if they are unpeeled. A recipe for 50 portions requires six pounds of cooked shrimp. Twelve pounds of raw shrimp or 10 pounds of raw, peeled, deveined shrimp produce six pounds cooked.

1.   **What are these variations costing the organization?**
2.   **How can Janet resolve these problems?**

ROAST BEEF RUN-OUT
Worksheet 7 Managing Food Production

Sharon Hagley, RD, the clinical nutrition manager in a 500 bed hospital, routinely visited the patient tray line during lunch operations to see how things were going. The tray line normally ran from 11:30 to 12:45 although the FSD wanted the line to finish at 12:30. There were ten positions on the tray line.

When Sharon arrived at 12:35 there were still two floors to serve (65 trays) and everyone on the tray line was standing around doing nothing.

Sharon asked the supervisor, Jim Bunting, "What is going on? Why aren't we finished?"

Jim responded, "Well, we ran out of roast beef which is running on the regulars and most of the modified diets. I counted all of the menus coming up and I need 44 portions."

"What are you doing about it?" Sharon inquired. "We have 65 patients not getting lunch, 10 people down here standing around and tray passers on the floor who have nothing to pass. Looks like the cooks are working on this problem and not preparing the supper meal. This isn't good."

"I know, I know," Jim said. "The cooks are looking for a substitue item. I think we can use 30 portions of veal roast left over from last night and we'll pull 15 hamburgers from the cafeteria to round it out. It will take 15 minutes to slice and re-heat the veal and and then we can re-start the tray line."

"So when do you think the tray line will finish?" asked Sharon.

"Well, we'll get started by 12:50. It will take about 30 minutes to finish up the line. Say 1:20," replied Jim.

"Guess we better notify the nursing stations about the delay. We are going to have some unhappy patients today. Leftovers and hamburgers were not what they expected to receive," commented Sharon.

What has happened in this operation?

Part two to be provided by the instructor.

JUNE JACKSON'S REQUEST
Worksheet 4 The Menu
Worksheet 7 Managing Food Production

When Irene Maiwald, supervisor of foodservice for Pleasant Valley School District, was visiting Thomas Jefferson School (grades 4-6) she was approached by June Jackson, R.N., the school nurse. June said, "I'm so glad I ran into you. I have been thinking about calling you to discuss a concern I have. I am finding that a number of our students come to school without eating breakfast. When children are hungry it really makes it difficult for them to pay attention and learn."

Irene responded, "You're right. I've been aware that there are some children who don't seem to have anyone to provide breakfast at home, or who just get up too late to eat, or have other situations which prevent them from eating before they come. Do you have a sense of how big the problem is?"

June said, "Not really. I've heard from quite a few of the teachers that they have noticed from 2 to 5 students in each class seem to be hungry many mornings. I could do a survey although I am reluctant to embarrass the children by asking them directly. I suspect that between 15 to 30% of the students on any given day have not had breakfast before arriving at school. (See Table 1 for students in Pleasant Valley School district.)

Irene was surprised. "I didn't realize the problem was that widespread. I'll look into what would be involved in offering breakfast in the cafeteria."

As Irene though about offering breakfast she could think of some potential problems. The school day began at 8:30 with home room and then classes started at 9:00. School busses arrived between 8:20 and 8:30 although some students walked to school. The doors were opened at 8:30 to let the students in.

Teachers were unionized and represented by the National Education Association (NEA). The labor contract with NEA indicated that working hours for teachers began at 8:30. The contract allowed for teachers to supervise the cafeteria during the lunch period. Students were not admitted to school before 8:30 because they would not be supervised by teachers any earlier.

Irene knew that other schools which offered breakfast had utilized their own employees to produce and serve the meal. Normally they had one employee for 80 students, two employees for 80 to 100 students and 3 employees for 100 students or more. School breakfast programs are encouraged by attractive reimbursement rates offered by the Federal government. (See breakfast reimbursement rates Table 2.)

Irene began to consider the menu for a breakfast program. She did not think a cold breakfast every day was appropriate, but she wasn't certain that the staff could manage a hot meal each day. She decided that, if they were going to implement breakfast, two hot meals per week and three cold would be a good way to start.

If Irene decides to go forward with this idea she needs a good plan that would consider a number of variables.

Should Irene begin a School Breakfast program at Thomas Jefferson school?

Table 1:   **Students in Pleasant Valley School District**

Schools	Number	Grades	Students per school	Total Students	% eating lunch
High School - Ray Kroc	1	9-12	1100	1100	75
Middle Schools	2	7-8	300	600	45
Upper Elementary	3	4-6	300	900	80
Lower Elementary	5	k-3	240	1200	80

Table 2:   **Reimbursement Rates for School Breakfast Programs**

	Paid by student	Paid by Federal Government
Paid meals	$ .45	$ .19
Reduced price meals	.25	1.05
Free meals	0	1.35

Table 3:   **Wages and Benefits Paid**

Position	Rate per hour
Cook/manager	$ 9.50
Cook	7.50
Cold preparation	6.50
Service	6.00

RAY KROC HIGH SCHOOL
Worksheet 7 Managing Food Production

Irene Maiwald, supervisor of foodservice at the Pleasant Valley School District has decided to develop a commissary/satellite food system using three schools as "cooking schools." The rest of the schools will receive prepared foods from the cooking schools and serve the finished product to the students. She has decided that the food for the high school and the two middle schools will be prepared at Ray Kroc High School. The menu for the high school is similar to that for the middle schools except that the middle schools have a prepared salad and prepared sandwich each day and no salad bar or deli bar. (See menu.)

In all schools records are maintained of the number of students who selected the various options for each menu item. (See demand records Table 1.)

As Irene considers consolidating cooking into three schools, she recognizes that all eleven schools will need to be renovated.

1. **Considering a commissary/satellite production system, develop a production sheet for Ray Kroc foodservice staff for Wednesday. How many portions of each product should be prepared?** (Use Food Production Record, pg. 115)
2. **Develop an equipment list for Ray Kroc High School including number and size. Develop the specifications for one piece of equipment. Indicate whether it is a partial or complete specification.**

MENU

Menu Item	Monday	Tuesday	Wednesday	Thursday	Friday
Hot Entrée Choice	Chicken Nuggets w/Sweet & Sour Sauce & Wheat Roll	Hot Dog on Roll w/ Condiments	Chicken in a basket w/oven baked fries & Whole Wheat Roll	Hamburger or Cheeseburger on Roll & Condiments	Tuna Melt
	French Bread Pizza	Beef or Pork Burrito	Calzone w/ Vegetables & Cheese	Macaroni & Cheese w/ Whole Wheat Roll	Mushroom Pizza w/ Bread Sticks
With	Pasta Salad with broccoli	Mexican Corn	Green Beans	Tossed Salad w/ Low Fat Dressing	Vegetable sticks w/ Cucumber Dill Sauce
OR Salad Bar	Turkey Salad Mixed Greens Raisins Sliced Cucumbers	Tuna Salad Mixed Greens Sliced Eggs Cherry Tomatoes	Egg Salad Mixed Greens Garbanzo Beans Broccoli	Chicken Salad Mixed Greens Chow Mein Noodles Spinach Leaves	Ham Salad Mixed Greens Sunflower Seeds Cauliflower
OR Deli (Choice of bread or roll	Tuna Salad Lettuce and Tomato	Ham Swiss Cheese Lettuce and Tomato	American Sub Provolone Cheese Lettuce and Tomato	Turkey American Cheese Lettuce and Tomato	Roast Beef Monterrey Jack Lettuce and Tomato
And Dessert Choice And Beverage	Fresh Fruit Ice Cream 1% Milk	Pineapple Chunks Oatmeal/Raisin Cookie 1% Milk	Chocolate Pudding Apple 1% Milk	Sliced Pears Cookie 1% Milk	Peach Cobbler Frozen Fruit Dessert 1% Milk

Table 1:	Demand Records								
Menu Item	sept	oct	nov	dec	jan	feb	mar	apr	**may**

RAY KROC

Menu Item	sept	oct	nov	dec	jan	feb	mar	apr	may
calzones	137	156	195	151	212	190	203	196	
chicken in a basket	210	231	238	275	260	240	192	205	
green beans	190	215	220	286	293	210	200	225	
salad bar	365	310	290	261	273	265	313	311	
deli bar	198	190	171	153	145	165	130	171	
chocolate pudding	702	634	577	491	528	585	635	709	
fresh apple	208	265	317	349	362	275	203	174	

THOMAS DEWEY MIDDLE SCHOOL

Menu Item	sept	oct	nov	dec	jan	feb	mar	apr	may
calzones	47	42	44	45	39	36	29	22	
chicken in a basket	28	30	35	47	50	47	44	35	
green beans	30	33	48	51	54	52	48	36	
egg salad plate	20	24	18	10	11	13	16	34	
American sub	43	38	42	37	31	34	42	49	
chocolate pudding	78	69	68	61	56	89	88	93	
fresh apple	60	65	71	78	75	41	43	47	

ADMIRAL FARRAGUT MIDDLE SCHOOL

Menu Item	sept	oct	nov	dec	jan	feb	mar	apr	may
calzones	49	40	46	43	41	39	31	20	
chicken in a basket	30	28	37	45	52	48	46	33	
green beans	37	35	44	56	60	48	51	43	
egg salad plate	22	22	20	8	13	11	18	32	
American sub	45	36	44	35	33	32	44	47	
chocolate pudding	75	68	65	52	83	86	94	82	
fresh apple	71	58	82	79	56	44	45	50	

DAVID BEDFORD
Worksheet 8 Meal Service

David is developing a business plan for the hospital administrator that argues strongly for a complete renovation of production and service facilities. The current operation provides tray service for 650 patients per day and cafeteria service for staff which numbers over 2000. Not all staff eat in the cafeteria because it only seats 250 and becomes very crowded at lunch time. David also provides catered meals when there are medical, nursing, or other conferences and meetings. David would like to be able to service hospital visitors and outpatients in the renovated facility. He also thinks that it would be important to offer 24 hour foodservice for staff without keeping the cafeteria open. The current cafeteria hours are 6:00 A.M. to 7:30 P.M. which means that night staff are not able to be served. David would like to have a really nice facility for staff and visitors so that he can keep these meal dollars in house. It annoys him to see a pizza delivery vehicle pull up to the hospital lobby to provide an evening meal for staff.

The current production system is a conventional system with most food prepared on-site. David has a CIA trained chef in charge of production, John Jeffries. John has done an excellent job in up-grading food quality by standardizing the recipes and thoroughly training the foodservice staff. John along with the rest of the department staff have frequently discussed the type of production they would like to have in the new facility. They have decided on a static menu for patient service with a cook-chill production system. They plan to develop a five week cycle menu for the cafeteria using cook-chill technology as much as possible. They think that display cooking in the cafeteria might work along with a scatter system, although they have not ruled out a food court or marche' operation.

Now they need to develop plans for the various food delivery systems which should be considered.

1. Develop a plan which describes how the food would be delivered and served to patients, staff and visitors, and catering.
2. Are there any other customers who could be served and how could they be managed?

SANDY DRAKE
Worksheet 8 Meal Service

A recent internship graduate, Sandy Drake was excited about her new position in a mid-sized tertiary care hospital. Sandy expected to work as a clinical dietitian while pursuing further education and becoming both a CDE and earning an MS in nutrition education. Sandy's internship had been quite good and she had enjoyed most of the rotations except for food production. She could not really see how working in the kitchen would help her to be a diabetes educator.

Helen Aimes, Sandy's CNM, came to her with a new assignment. "I want you to start checking the patient tray line at breakfast each morning that you are here. We've been having some complaints and I'd like to get things squared away quickly."

"I'm not sure what I can do about it," said Sandy. "I thought you wanted me to be a clinical dietitian. How will checking the tray line help me to see all of my patients? You expect me to see 15 patients each day and it will be hard for me to maintain that level and check breakfast as well."

Helen agreed, "I know the additional responsibility comes at a difficult time. Have you noticed that there is a lot of plate waste on the patient trays?"

"Not really," replied Sandy. "I guess I haven't paid much attention to their intake. I have been focusing on their lab values and drug-nutrient interactions. I have been recommending nutritional supplements frequently."

"I have noticed that we are increasing our use of supplements," said Helen. "Perhaps if the patients enjoyed their meals more supplement use would decrease. What do you think?"

Sandy could not disagree.

1.   **Recommend what Sandy should do about the breakfast tray line.**
2.   **What else would you recommend to this foodservice operation?**

Part two to be provided by the instructor.

SPRING HILLS SENIOR CENTER
Worksheet 5 Purchasing, Receiving, and Inventory Control
Worksheet 6 Food Production Methods
Worksheet 8 Meal Service

A special luncheon was planned for the tenth anniversary of the Spring Hills Senior Center. The participant advisory committee made recommendations about the menu which was to feature foods popular with the participants. The menu would be served both at the senior center and through HDM. Reservations were being accepted and the expected number was 375 on site and 138 through HDM.

MENU

Fresh Fruit Cup (3 oz) with Mint Sprig
Roast Pork Loin (3 oz) garnished with Candied Apple Ring
Gravy
Baked Potatoes with Chive Sour Cream
Steamed Broccoli (3 oz)
Tossed Vegetable Salad (½ cup) (Lettuce, Shred Carrots, Cuc, Tomatoes)
Thousand Island Dressing (2 Tbsp)
Parker House Roll and Butter
Blueberry Cobbler(3 oz) w/ Whipped Cream
Low Fat Milk (1 cup)

1. Develop a purchase order for this luncheon. (Use Purchase Order, pg. 117.)
2. Develop a specification for the baking potato.
3. Develop a production sheet for the luncheon. (Use Food Production Record, pg. 115.)
4. Develop service recommendations for this meal.

97

JEFF JORDAN
Worksheet 9 Financial Management and Cost Control

The new director of foodservices for the Evergreen Computer Company, Jeff Jordan, has some real concerns. He was hired to turn around the foodservice operation which was experiencing major financial difficulties. Upper level management noticed that the net profit of the foodservice operation had dropped from nearly $40,000 in the first quarter to less than $15,000 in the fourth quarter in spite of rising sales. Jeff's job is to identify the problem and fix it.

As Jeff analyzed the profit and loss statement (see next page) it became clear that the item which was rising the fastest was cost of goods sold. This increase was occurring in an environment where the cost of living had increased by 2.5% on an annual basis. Cost of goods sold includes the cost of food used to produce meals. Controllable expenses which includes salaries and wages, employee benefits, direct operating expenses, energy and utility service, administrative and general expenses, and repairs and maintenance had increased but still constituted 47% of the income from sales. Jeff considered controllable expenses to be under good control. The previous director had thought that an appropriate strategy to increase net income was to increase prices for meals. Upper level management did not view raising prices favorably if there was any other way to avoid losses. The company provided the space for the foodservice rent free and they believed that there should be some profits accruing to the organization. The way things were going it looked as if the next quarter could show a loss in net income.

Evergreen Computer Company is both the headquarters, the major manufacturing location, and the warehouse for a computer firm which produces both personal computers and software to support business applications. There are approximately 1100 employees in the headquarters building with another 1200 employees in manufacturing facility and warehouse. Food is prepared in the main kitchen in the headquarters and is served there in a cafeteria as well as in several satellite cafeterias scattered throughout the complex. There are also a number of mobile carts which provide food for coffee breaks and light snacks in a variety of areas. The mobile carts carry a cash drawer to accept payment for products sold.

Food costs are determined by adding up all costs of food received plus the beginning inventory. The ending inventory is subtracted to provide the cost of food used during the time period. (See inventory reconciliation.)

The production manager routinely submits requisitions to the storeroom for needed ingredients and supplies. These are delivered to the production area on a daily basis. Jeff noticed that the storage facilities are not always locked. Additionally when ingredients are forgotten, production staff go to the storage area and pick up needed items. There are many doors in and out of the various production and service units through which people can pass at will. The cashiers in all of the cafeterias are long time employees who use POS registers. They have many friends among the employees of the computer firm whom they greet by name and engage in conversation.

The receiving and storage systems are completely computerized so that a perpetual inventory is maintained. The purchasing manager uses the perpetual inventory to order. Frequently, however, products that are listed as available in the computer are not found in the storage facilities. A physical inventory is conducted once each quarter to verify the perpetual inventory. (See inventory reconciliation.) When Jeff compared the physical inventory with the requisitions there was shrinkage of over $54,000 in three months.

How can Jeff improve net income?

Profit and Loss Statement

	1st quarter	2nd quarter	3rd quarter	4th quarter
Sales	$760,518.00	$771,144.00	$780,252.00	$787,842.00
- Cost of goods sold	325,501.78	341,850.66	355,448.87	378,765.35
= Gross profit	435,016.22	429,293.34	424,803.13	409,076.65
- Controllable expenses	357,443.40	362,437.60	366,718.40	370,285.70
= Income before interest and depreciation	77,572.82	66,855.74	58,084.73	38,790.95
- Interest	7,605.18	7,605.18	7,605.18	7,605.18
- Depreciation	9,126.20	9,126.20	9,126.20	9,126.20
= Income before taxes	60,840.44	50,124.36	41,353.35	22,059.57
- Taxes	21,294.29	17,543.53	14,473.67	7,720.85
= Net income	$ 39,546.29	$ 32,580.83	$ 26,879.68	$ 14,338.72

Inventory Reconciliation

Value of inventory on 1 October	$ 3,500.00
+ Food purchases (Oct - Dec)	379,965.35
= Cost of food available	382,965.35
- Inventory on 1 January	4,200.00
= Cost of food used	378,765.35
- Cost of direct & requisition issues	323,996.93
= Difference	$ 54,768.42

REFERENCES

REFERENCES
References listed by date of publication.

References for each problem will be suggested by your instructor. This reference list is provided as an additional source which you may wish to consult.

School Lunch

Luck J, Cazier A. *Food Purchasing Pointers for School Food Service*. Washington, DC: Nutrition and Technical Services Staff, Food and Nutrition Service, US Dept. of Agriculture; 1977

Manka AM, Turetsky JR, Binzer MC, Brodeur MP. *Quantity Recipes for School Food Service*. Washington, DC: Nutrition and Technical Services Division, US Dept. of Agriculture; 1988.

American Heart Association. *The Healthy School Lunch Menus*. Dallas, Texas. American Heart Association; 1992.

VanEgmond-Pannell D. *Cost Control Manual for School Food Service Directors in Massachusetts*. Framingham, Massachusetts: Massachusetts Department of Education; 1993.

Design Handbook. Alabama: State Department of Education; 1994.

Brown N, Dana J , Gilmore S, Brooke A. *Food Quality Evaluation and Assurance Manual for School Food Service.* Hattiesburg, Mississippi: National Food Service Management Institute; 1995.

Gunn M. *First Choice: A Purchasing System Manual School Food Service*. University of Mississippi: National Food Service Management Institute; 1995.

Luoto PK, Plummer PF. *Menu Planning Project: Implementation of the Dietary Guidelines in School Food Programs*. Framingham, Massachusetts: John C. Stalker Institute of Food and Nutrition; 1995.

National school lunch program and school breakfast program: school meals initiative for healthy children (7CFR 219, 220). *Federal Register*. June 13, 1995;60:31188-31222.

Assisted NuMenus. School breakfast and school lunch menus. Washington, DC Food and Consumer Service, Nutrition and Technical Services Division. US Dept. of Agriculture; 1996.

Robinson A, Kidd J, Ford S, Bogle S. *Culinary Techniques for Healthy School Meals* (video series). University of Mississippi: National Food Service Management Institute; 1996.

Martin J., Conklin M. (editors). *Managing for Excellence: Child Nutrition Programs for the 21st Century.* Maryland: In Press: Aspen Publishers, 1999.

VanEgmond-Pannell D. *School Foodservice*, 5th ed. Westport, CT: AVI Publishing; 1999.

Food Production Techniques

Kotschevar LH. *Standards, Principles and Techniques in Quantity Food Production*, 4th ed. NY: Van Nostrand Reinhold; 1988.

Cracknell HL. *The New Catering Repertoire*. NY: Van Nostrand Reinhold; 1989.

Breeding C, Foster D. *Cost-Effective Recipes for 10 to 100*. NY: Van Nostrand Reinhold; 1989.

Knight JB, Kotschevar LH. *Quantity Food Production, Planning and Management*. NY: Van Nostrand Reinhold; 1989.

McCormack MK: *Creative Quantity Cooking*, Rockville, MD: Aspen Publications; 1989.

Terrell ME, Headlund DB. *Large Quantity Recipes*, 4th ed. NY: Van Nostrand Reinhold; 1989

Kittler PG. *International Quantity Foods*. NY: Van Nostrand Reinhold; 1990.

Light ND, Walker A. *Cook-Chill Catering: Technology and Management*. NY: Elsevier Applied Science; 1990.

Ruffel D. *The Professional Caterer Series*. NY: Van Nostrand Reinhold; 1990.

Turner S, Aronowitz V. *Heartwise Quantity Cookbook*. Center for Science in the Public Interest; 1990.

Dawson H. *Great Food for Great Numbers*. NY: Van Nostrand Reinhold; 1991.

Fuller J, Renold E. *The Chef's Compendium of Professional Recipes*, 3rd ed. Oxford; Boston: Butterworth and Heinemann; 1992.

Messersmith A, Miller J. *Forecasting in Food Service*. NY: Wiley; 1992.

Gisslen W: *Advanced Professional Cooking*. NY: Wiley; 1992.

Donovan MD, editor. *The Professional Chef's Techniques of Healthy Cooking*. NY: Van Nostrand Reinhold; 1993.

Holden C. *Cooking for Fifty: The Complete Reference and Cookbook*. NY: Wiley; 1993.

Gisslen W. *Professional Baking*. NY: Wiley; 1994.

Caserani V. *Advanced Practical Cookery*. London: Hodder & Stoughton; 1995.

Frank S. *Menu Solutions: Quantity Recipes for Regular and Special Diets*. NY: Wiley; 1996.

Gisslen W: *Professional Cooking*, 3rd ed., NY: Wiley; 1995.

Kapoor S. *Professional Healthy Cooking*. NY: Wiley; 1995.

The Moosewood Restaurant Cooks for a Crowd: Recipes with a Vegetarian Emphasis for 24 or More. NY: Wiley; 1996.

Culinary Institute of America. *The New Professional Chef*, 6th ed. NY: Van Nostrand Reinhold; 1996.

Molt M. *Food for Fifty*, 10th ed. Upper Saddle River, NJ: Prentice Hall, Inc.; 1997.

Menu Planning

Wenzel GL. *Wenzel's Menu Maker*, 2nd ed. NY, CBI Publishing; 1979.

Eckstein EF. *Menu Planning*, 3rd ed. Westport, CT: AVI Publishing; 1983

Kreck LA. *Menus Analysis and Planning*, 2nd ed. Boston MA: CBI Publishing; 1984.

Kotschevar LH. *Management by Menu*, 2nd ed. Chicago, IL: National Institute for the Foodservice Industry; 1987.

Hodges CA. *Culinary Nutrition for Foodservice Professionals*, NY: Van Nostrand Reinhold; 1989.

Ganen BC. *Nutritional Menu Concepts for the Hospitality Industry*, NY: Van Nostrand Reinhold; 1990.

McVety PJ. *Fundamentals of Menu Planning*. NY: Van Nostrand Reinhold; 1990.

Seaberg AG. *Menu Design: Merchandising and Marketing*. NY: Van Nostrand Reinhold; 1991.

Splaver BR. *Successful Catering*, 3rd ed. NY: Van Nostrand Reinhold; 1991.

Scanlon NL. *Catering Menu Management*, NY: Wiley; 1992.

Drysdale JA. *Profitable Menu Planning*. Englewood Cliffs, NJ: Prentice Hall; 1994.

Drummond KE. *Nutrition for the Foodservice Professional*, 3rd ed. NY: Van Nostrand Reinhold; 1997.

Purchasing, Ordering, and Specifications

Matthews RH, Garrison YJ. *Food Yields Summarized by Different Stages of Preparation*. (US Dept of Agriculture Handbook 102); 1975.

Batcher PM. *Food Purchasing Guide for Group Feeding*. USDA, Human Nutrition Information Service; 1983.

Pedderson RB. *Foodservice and Hotel Purchasing*. New York: Van Nostrand Reinhold; 1983.

Warfel MC, Cremer ML. *Purchasing for Foodservice Managers*. Berkeley, CA: McCutchan Publishing; 1985.

US Food and Nutrition Services. *Guidelines for the Storage and Care of Food Products.* Food Industry Group and USDA; 1987.

Nixon JA. *Contract Purchasing: A Manual for Foodservice Supervisors*, 2nd ed. Silver Spring, MD: Food Information Service Center; 1989.

deHoll JF. *Encyclopedia of Labeling for Meat and Poultry, 9th ed*. 1989. St. Louis, MO: *Meat Plant Magazine*, 9701 Gravois Ave, St. Louis MO 63123

Coltman MM. *Hospitality Industry Purchasing*. NY: Van Nostrand Reinhold; 1990.

Stefanelli JM. *Purchasing, Selection and Procurement for the Hospitality Industry*, 3rd ed. NY: Wiley; 1992.

Trends: School Food Service in the Year 2000 and Beyond. (Conference proceedings) Sneed J, editor. 1992. National Food Service Management Institute. P.O. Drawer 188, University MS 38677-0188.

Building for the Future: Nutrition Guidance for the Child Nutrition Program (FNS-279), US Dept. of Agriculture; April 1992.

The Meat Buyers Guide. 1992. National Association of Meat Purveyors, 1920 Association Drive., Suite 400, Reston VA 22091-1547.

Reed L. *SPECS, The Comprehensive Foodservice Purchasing and Specification Manual*. NY: Van Nostrand Reinhold; 1993.

Kotschevar LH, Donnelly R. *Quantity Food Purchasing*, 4th ed. NY: Macmillian; 1994.

Robertson K. *Purchasing for Foodservice*. Ames, IA: Iowa State University; 1994.

National Food Service Management Institute. *Choice Plus: A Reference Guide for Foods and Ingredients*. USDA, Food and Consumer Service. Publication Number FCS-297; 1996.

The Buying Guide for Fresh Fruits, Vegetables, Herbs, and Nuts. Blue Goose Growers, Inc. P.O. box M, Shepherdstown, WV 25443.

American Heart Association and the Massachusetts School Food Service Association. *Choose the Right Stuff*. American Heart Association, Massachusetts Affiliate, Inc., 20 Speen St., Framingham, MA, 01701.

Statewide Cooperative Purchasing Program, State of Montana. Gary Watt, School Food Services, Office of Public Instruction, The Capitol Building, Helena, MT 59620.

Manuals for food service supervisors. Food Information Service Center, 21050 SW 93rd Lane Road, Dunnellon FL 32630
      Vol 1. *Catalog of Specifications*
      Vol 2. *Contract Purchasing*
      Vol 3. *Food Facts*
      Vol 4. *Directory of Information Sources*
      Vol 5. *Storage and Care of Food Products*
      Vol 6. *Purchasing French Fry Potatoes*
      Vol 7. *USDA Donated Foods Program*
      Vol 8. *Guidelines for Food Purchasing and Meal Cost Management* (schools and institutions)
      Vol 9. *Guidelines for Food Purchasing and Meal Cost Management* (nutrition programs for the elderly)
      Vol 10. *Food Identifications and Standards*

Sanitation and Safety

Longree K, Blaker GG. *Sanitary Techniques in Food Service*, 2nd ed. NY: Wiley; 1982.

Minor LJ. *Sanitation, Safety and Environmental Standards*, vol 2. Westport, CN: AVI Publishing; 1983.

Guthrie RK. *Food Sanitation*, 3rd ed. NY: Van Nostrand Reinhold; 1988.

Salmonellosis Control: The Role of Animal and Product Hygiene. WHO Technical Report Series; 1988.

Jacob M. *Safe Food Handling: A Training Guide for Managers of Food Service Establishments*. Geneva: WHO; 1989.

Dykstra JJ. *Infection Control for Lodging and Food Service Establishments*. NY: Wiley; 1990.

Bryan FL. *Hazard Analysis Critical Control Point Evaluation*. Geneva: WHO; 1992.

Guthrie RK. *Salmonella*. Boca Raton, FL: CRC Press; 1992.

Hayes PR. *Food Microbiology and Hygiene*, 2nd ed. London & NY: Elsevier Applied Science; 1992.

Educational Foundation of the National Restaurant Association. *Applied Foodservice Sanitation*, 4th ed. NY: Wiley; 1992.

Cichy RF. *Sanitation Management*, 2nd ed. East Lansing, MI: Educational Institute of the American Hotel and Motel Association; 1993.

Hobbs BC. *Food Poisoning and Food Hygiene*, 6th ed. Baltimore MD: Edward Arnold; 1993.

National Assessment Institute. *Handbook for Safe Foodservice Management*. Englewood Cliffs, NJ: Prentice Hall; 1994.

Lachney A. *The HACCP Cookbook and Manual*. Eatonville, WA: Nutrition Development Systems; 1996.

Longree K, Armbruster G. *Quantity Food Sanitation*, 5th ed. NY: Wiley; 1996.

Foodborne Disease Surveillance, Annual Summary. Center for Disease Control.

Foodservice Equipment

National Sanitation Foundation. *NSF Food Service Equipment Standards*. Ann Arbor, MI: The Foundation; 1978.

Wilkinson J. *The Complete Book of Cooking Equipment*, 2nd ed. Boston, MA: CBI Publishing; 1981.

Hospital Patient Feeding Systems: Proceedings of a symposium held at Raddison South Hotel, Minneapolis, MN. October 19-21, 1981. Washington: National Academy Press; 1982.

Avery A. *A Modern Guide to Foodservice Equipment*. Boston, MA: CBI Publishing; 1985.

Kotschevar LH, Terrell ME. *Foodservice Planning: Layout and Equipment*, 3rd ed. NY: Wiley; 1985.

Greaves RE. *The Commercial Food Equipment Repair and Maintenance Manual*, NY: CBI Publishing; 1987.

Jernigan AK. *Foodservice Equipment*. Ames, IA: University Press; 1989.

Scriven C, Stevens J. *Food Equipment Facts*, NY: Wiley; 1989.

Stevens JW, Scriven C. *Manual of Equipment and Design for the Foodservice Industry*. NY: Van Nostrand Reinhold; 1989.

Quality Control

Thorner M, Manning PB. *Quality Control in Foodservice*, revised ed. Westport, CT: AVI Publishing; 1983.

Tolve AP. *Standardizing Foodservice for Quality and Efficiency*. Westport, CT: AVI Publishing; 1984.

Klein BP, Matthews ME, Setser CS. *Foodservice Systems: Time and Temperature Effects on Food Quality*. North Central Regional Research Publication No. 293, Illinois Bulletin 779. Agriculture Experiment Station, College of Agriculture, University of Illinois at Urbana-Champaign; 1984.

Renner-McCaffrey J, LeyShon AH. *Quality Assurance in Hospital Nutrition Services*. Rockville, MD: Aspen Publishing; 1988.

Ruf KL. *Quality Control, Quality Assurance: Manual for Food and Nutrition*. Rockville, MD: Aspen Publishing; 1989.

Contract Food Service

Zaccarelli HE, Ninermeier JD. *Cost Effective Contract Food Service*. Rockville,MD: Aspen Publishing; 1982.

Warner M. *Noncommercial, Institutional, and Contract Food Service Management*. NY: Wiley; 1994.

Information Systems

Kasavana, ML. *Computer Systems for Foodservice Operations*. NY: Van Nostrand Reinhold; 1984.

Chaban J. *Practical Foodservice Spreadsheets with Lotus 1-2-3*, 2nd ed. NY: Van Nostrand Reinhold; 1994.

Pappas MJ. *Eat Food, Not Profits!! How Computers Can Save your Restaurant*. NY: Van Nostrand Reinhold; 1997.

Miscellaneous

Rose JC, editor. *Handbook for Health Care Food Service Management*. Rockville, MD: Aspen Publishing; 1984.

Knight's Foodservice Dictionary, NY: Van Nostrand Reinhold; 1987.

Bakos JB, Karrick GE, editors. *Dining in Corporate America*. Rockville, MD: Aspen Publishing; 1989.

Byers BA, Shanklin CW, Hoover LC. *Food Service Manual for Health Care Institutions*. Chicago, IL: American Hospital Publishing; 1994.

FORMS FOR PROBLEMS

FOOD PRODUCTION RECORD

Cycle Week:
Day:
Date:

Organization:
Participants:
Weather/Other Factors:

LUNCH MENU

Menu Item	Cooking equipment	Portion size	Portions forecast	Portions prepared	Left over	Portions used	Comments

Problems:

Ray Kroc
Spring Hills

Purchase Order

Menu Item	Quantity Needed	Purchase Quantity	Comments

©Lieux & Luoto. *Exploring Quantity Food Production and Service through Problems*

Problem: Spring Hills Senior Center

EVALUATION FORMS

PROBLEM WRITE-UP EVALUATION

GROUP_____ PROBLEM_____ REPORTER_____

Identification of Learning Issues. (Completeness, depth, pertinence)

Points

Discussion of Learning Issues. (Analysis, comprehensiveness, documentation of resources, conclusion, overall excellence of discussion)

Points

Quality of Report. (Writing style, grammar, usage, logical development, spelling, presentation)

Points

Total points

SUBMIT WITH EACH WRITE UP. WRITEUPS WILL NOT BE RETURNED.

121

PROBLEM WRITE-UP EVALUATION

GROUP_____ PROBLEM_____ REPORTER_____

Identification of Learning Issues. (Completeness, depth, pertinence)

Points

Discussion of Learning Issues. (Analysis, comprehensiveness, documentation of resources, conclusion, overall excellence of discussion)

Points

Quality of Report. (Writing style, grammar, usage, logical development, spelling, presentation)

Points

Total points

SUBMIT WITH EACH WRITE UP. WRITEUPS WILL NOT BE RETURNED.

PROBLEM WRITE-UP EVALUATION

GROUP_____ PROBLEM_____ REPORTER_____

Identification of Learning Issues. (Completeness, depth, pertinence)

Points

Discussion of Learning Issues. (Analysis, comprehensiveness, documentation of resources, conclusion, overall excellence of discussion)

Points

Quality of Report. (Writing style, grammar, usage, logical development, spelling, presentation)

Points

Total points

SUBMIT WITH EACH WRITE UP. WRITEUPS WILL NOT BE RETURNED.

125

CRITERIA FOR EVALUATION OF STUDENT PERFORMANCE IN GROUP TASKS

PARTICIPATION

DOES NOT MEET EXPECTATIONS: Rarely speaks, quiet; little effort to contribute to group learning in other ways (e.g. bring in readings). OR Disrupts group with unhelpful or irrelevant comments, dominates discussions.

MEETS EXPECTATIONS: Contributes regularly by asking questions, generating hypotheses, sharing information, contributing learning resources; does not dominate or intimidate.

EXCEEDS EXPECTATIONS: Takes the lead in discussion and moving the group learning forward. Facilitates participation of fellow group members.

PREPARATION

DOES NOT MEET EXPECTATIONS: Frequently unprepared. Little evidence of reading or independent study. Fails to follow through with self-directed learning tasks.

MEETS EXPECTATIONS: Consistently prepared. Shows evidence of reading and self-directed study.

EXCEEDS EXPECTATIONS: Demonstrates high level of preparation beyond that minimally required for problem. Takes initiative to find high quality resources.

KNOWLEDGE ACQUISITION

DOES NOT MEET EXPECTATIONS: Displays limited knowledge acquisition; consistently unable to answer questions.

MEETS EXPECTATIONS: Demonstrates basic comprehension of facts and principles; able to answer most questions.

EXCEEDS EXPECTATIONS: Demonstrates excellent command of facts and principles; answers to questions and volunteered explanations show insight and understanding.

REASONING PROCESSES, COMMUNICATION, AND ABILITY TO SYNTHESIZE AND APPLY INFORMATION

DOES NOT MEET EXPECTATIONS: Consistently has difficulty identifying problems, generating hypotheses, drawing conclusions, and seeing the "big picture." Explanations illogical or poorly formulated. Unable to integrate and synthesize information. Has difficulty applying facts and principles to problems.

MEETS EXPECTATIONS: Consistently able to identify problems, generate and test reasonable hypotheses, and draw reasonable and well formulated conclusions from the data. Communicates ideas clearly. Able to generalize for the specifics and displays ability to apply information to new problems.

EXCEEDS EXPECTATIONS: Insightful, creative thinker. Presents logical and clearly formulated arguments. Outstanding ability to synthesize and integrate information. Has a knack for seeing the heart of a problem and for helping others achieve a higher level of reasoning. Able to apply facts and principles to new problems.

INTERPERSONAL SKILLS AND IMPROVEMENT

DOES NOT MEET EXPECTATIONS: Rude or disruptive. Displays poor listening skills. Insensitive to others and shows lack of respect. Defensive in response to criticism. Tardy; leaves early.

MEETS EXPECTATIONS: Considerate of group members. Listens well and avoids interrupting others. Shows respect and sensitivity to the feelings of others. Recognizes own strengths and weaknesses. Attends all sessions on time.

EXCEEDS EXPECTATIONS: Always considerate of group members and respectful of group process. Displays unusual perceptiveness and sensitivity to the feelings of others. Makes effort to facilitate participation by others; resolves conflicts. Responds to criticism gracefully; takes effective action to correct own weaknesses.

Criteria developed by John A. Sawyer, Ph.D., College of Business & Economics, University of Delaware, Newark DE.

ASSESSMENT OF INDIVIDUAL PERFORMANCE IN GROUPS

Names of Group Members A._____

B._____

C._____

D._____

E._____

Your Name _____

Use the following form to assess the contributions of everyone in your group including yourself. Using the following scale, rate each member of your group (A, B, C, D, E). Then rate yourself under the column "you." Use the criteria on page 129 to determine rating for each item.

		Does not meet expectations (1) (2)		Meets Expectations (3) (4)		Exceeds Expectations (5)	
	Criteria	A	B	C	D	E	you
1.	Participation	____	____	____	____	____	____
2.	Preparation	____	____	____	____	____	____
3.	Knowledge acquisition	____	____	____	____	____	____
4.	Reasoning, communication and ability to apply information	____	____	____	____	____	____
5.	Interpersonal skills and improvement	____	____	____	____	____	____

*A score of 1, 2, or 5 must be justified on the reverse side.

OVER

129

Additional comments on individuals indicating strengths and areas for improvement. Although these comments are anonymous, the instructor will provide feedback about the comments to each member of the group.

A.

B.

C.

D.

E.

you

ASSESSMENT OF INDIVIDUAL PERFORMANCE IN GROUPS

Names of Group Members A._____

B._____

C._____

D._____

E._____

Your Name _____

Use the following form to assess the contributions of everyone in your group including yourself. Using the following scale, rate each member of your group (A, B, C, D, E). Then rate yourself under the column "you." Use the criteria on page 129 to determine rating for each item.

		Does not meet expectations		Meets Expectations		Exceeds Expectations	
		(1)	(2)	(3)	(4)	(5)	
	Criteria	**A**	**B**	**C**	**D**	**E**	**you**
1.	**Participation**	____	____	____	____	____	____
2.	**Preparation**	____	____	____	____	____	____
3.	**Knowledge acquisition**	____	____	____	____	____	____
4.	**Reasoning, communication and ability to apply information**	____	____	____	____	____	____
5.	**Interpersonal skills and improvement**	____	____	____	____	____	____

*A score of 1, 2, or 5 must be justified on the reverse side.

OVER

131

Additional comments on individuals indicating strengths and areas for improvement. Although these comments are anonymous, the instructor will provide feedback about the comments to each member of the group.

A.

B.

C.

D.

E.

you

ASSESSMENT OF INDIVIDUAL PERFORMANCE IN GROUPS

Names of Group Members   A._____

B._____

C._____

D._____

E._____

Your Name   _____

Use the following form to assess the contributions of everyone in your group including yourself. Using the following scale, rate each member of your group (A, B, C, D, E). Then rate yourself under the column "you." Use the criteria on page 129 to determine rating for each item.

	Does not meet expectations (1) (2)	Meets Expectations (3) (4)	Exceeds Expectations (5)

	Criteria	A	B	C	D	E	you
1.	Participation	____	____	____	____	____	____
2.	Preparation	____	____	____	____	____	____
3.	Knowledge acquisition	____	____	____	____	____	____
4.	Reasoning, communication and ability to apply information	____	____	____	____	____	____
5.	Interpersonal skills and improvement	____	____	____	____	____	____

*A score of 1, 2, or 5 must be justified on the reverse side.

OVER

Additional comments on individuals indicating strengths and areas for improvement. Although these comments are anonymous, the instructor will provide feedback about the comments to each member of the group.

A. _____

B. _____

C. _____

D. _____

E. _____

you _____